MILLIKEN'S

COMPLETE BOOK OF

Grammar
REPRODUCIBLES

Over 110 Activities for Today's Differentiated Classroom

Compiled by: Sara Inskeep
Cover design: Logo Design Team
Page Layout: Janine M. Chambers

Printed in the United States of America

ISBN 978-1-4291-0461-6

MILLIKEN
P.O. Box 802 • Dayton, OH 45401
www.LorenzEducationalPress.com

How to Use This Book . . .

The activities in this book provide an excellent source of grammar practice for elementary students. The pages can be used as drill reinforcement or as independent instructional material and are designed to help motivate students to learn through a variety of exercises. The activities in this book are grouped by skill; these skills may overlap more than one grade level and should be used in ways that best meet each student's needs. The reproducibles are created so that a student can work with a minimum of supervision in a classroom or at home. Answer keys to all exercises have been provided in the back of the book.

EXTRA! EXTRA! When you see this symbol, be sure to check out the "extra" extension activity provided.

Table of Contents

Write the words that name **people** or **places** under the correct heading.
Draw a picture to go with each word.

boy   cat   man   home   mother
help   zoo   fun   store   go

People	Places

Cut out the pictures of **people** at the bottom of the page.
Paste the pictures in the **place** each should go.

Name _____ Date _____

Remember: A noun names a
person, place, or thing.

Write each word in the correct box below.

train	cow	store	boy	book
school	woman	car	library	zoo
baby	window	girl	park	man

PERSON...
1. _____
2. _____
3. _____
4. _____
5. _____

PLACE...
1. _____
2. _____
3. _____
4. _____
5. _____

THING...
1. _____
2. _____
3. _____
4. _____
5. _____

Use one word from each box in each sentence below.
Use your imagination!

1. The _____ lost a _____ in the _____ .

2. A _____ saw a _____ at the _____ .

3. The _____ took a _____ to the _____ .

On another sheet of paper, draw a picture of one of your funny sentences!

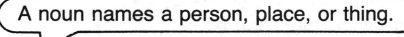

A noun names a person, place, or thing.

WORD BANK		
fish	bird	tail
feathers	eagles	nest

Complete each sentence with the correct noun. Use the word bank.

1. The bald eagle is our national _____ .

2. Its head is covered with white _____ .

3. Its _____ is also white.

4. The eagle builds its _____ in high places.

5. The bald eagle eats _____ .

On another sheet of paper, draw your own picture of a bald eagle.

Draw a line under the **singular** and **plural nouns.**
Draw a picture of the underlined noun in each sentence.

1. He got a present.

2. She likes her presents.

3. Blow up the balloons.

4. I like the big balloon.

5. Help me tie the ribbon.

Write a sentence about your best birthday present.

Nouns that tell about only one person, place, or thing are **singular**. Nouns that tell about more than one person, place, or thing are **plural**.

Example: **Singular** ⟶ bird   house   wave   boy
           Plural ⟶ birds   houses   waves   boys

Write each word where it belongs.

kite   monkeys   bats

letters   teacher   table

Singular   **Plural**

_____   _____

_____   _____

_____   _____

_____   _____

_____   _____

_____   _____

Circle the word that fits the picture.

book	car	sock
books	cars	socks

Singular nouns name one person, place, or thing.
Plural nouns name more than one person, place, or thing.

Put each word in the correct house.

babies	fox	book	giant
doll	women	cow	kites
bird	pennies	girls	coat
eggs	flags	gym	sleds

SINGULAR

PLURAL

Name _____ Date _____

Polly's
pointers:

A **plural noun** names more than one person, place, or thing. Most plural nouns are made by adding **s** to the **singular noun**. If a noun ends with **y** preceded by a consonant letter, change the **y** to **i** and add **es** to make a plural noun.

Write the plural of each singular noun in the blanks.

Arizona and New Mexico have many Indian _____. They are cliff
                                              pueblo
_____, built together like _____. One pueblo had 800 _____ and
house   apartment   room
housed many _____. Pueblo _____ were peaceful _____.
             family   tribe   farmer
They held _____ to pray for rain for their _____.
          ceremony   crop

Polly's
pointer:

If a noun ends with **sh**, **ch**, **x**, **s**, or **z**, add **es** to make the word **plural**.

Color each space in which the word could be made plural by adding **es**. If done correctly, you will learn the name of the Pueblo Indian's most important crop.

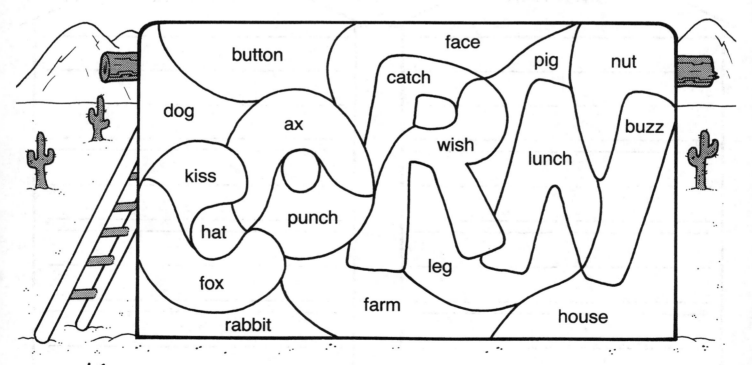

EXTRA!

On another sheet of paper, write the plurals of the words in the spaces that are not colored.

Add s to most nouns to mean more than one.

Make the nouns in ( ) plural.
Write the plural in each sentence.

1. The farmer planted _____ .
   (seed)

2. Pumpkins grew in the _____ .
   (field)

3. They grew on _____ .
   (vine)

4. Scarecrows kept the _____ away.
   (bird)

5. Now the _____ are ripe.
   (pumpkin)

Make a list of things that can be found on a farm.

Add **s** to each **noun** to make it **plural.** Write the noun. Draw a picture of each plural noun.

horn
_____
- - - - - - - - - -
_____

hat
_____
- - - - - - - - - -
_____

cake
_____
- - - - - - - - - -
_____

game
_____
- - - - - - - - - -
_____

toy
_____
- - - - - - - - - -
_____

EXTRA! Draw a picture of a plural noun found in the room.

Name _____ Date _____

An **exact noun** can make your writing better.

Look at the word in ( ) in each sentence. Find a more exact noun in the word bank. Write it on the line.

WORD BANK	stew	sofa	house
	Owls	brooms	cape

_____

1. The witch lives in an old (place) _____ .

2. (Birds) _____ live in the attic.

3. Her cat sleeps on the (furniture) _____ .

4. The witch hangs her (things) _____on the wall.

5. She cooks (food) _____ in a big pot.

6. The witch's (clothing) _____ is black.

Add **'s** to a noun to show who or what owns something.

Read the sentence pairs. Make the second sentence show who or what owns something. For example: The car belongs to Lew.

It is **Lew's** car.

1. The rattle belongs to the baby.

   _____

   ─ ─ ─ ─ ─ ─ ─ ─ ─ ─ ─ ─

   It is the _____ rattle.

2. The shell of the turtle is hard.

   _____

   ─ ─ ─ ─ ─ ─ ─ ─ ─ ─ ─ ─

   The _____ shell is hard.

3. The name of my sister is Judy.

   _____

   ─ ─ ─ ─ ─ ─ ─ ─ ─ ─ ─ ─

   My _____ name is Judy.

4. The tail of the beaver is flat.

   _____

   ─ ─ ─ ─ ─ ─ ─ ─ ─ ─ ─ ─

   The _____ tail is flat.

5. The hat belongs to Eric.

   _____

   ─ ─ ─ ─ ─ ─ ─ ─ ─ ─ ─ ─

   That is _____ hat.

Color each of the pictures above.

Name _____ Date _____

Remember:
A **verb** shows action. A **noun** names
a person, place, or thing.

Circle the **nouns** in red. Circle the verbs in purple.

city	kite	make	walk	book	run
man	glove	sleep	tree	banana	swim
see	zoo	eat	draw	paintbrush	go

Color each space that contains a **verb** blue. Color each space that
contains a **singular noun** yellow. Color **plural nouns** black.

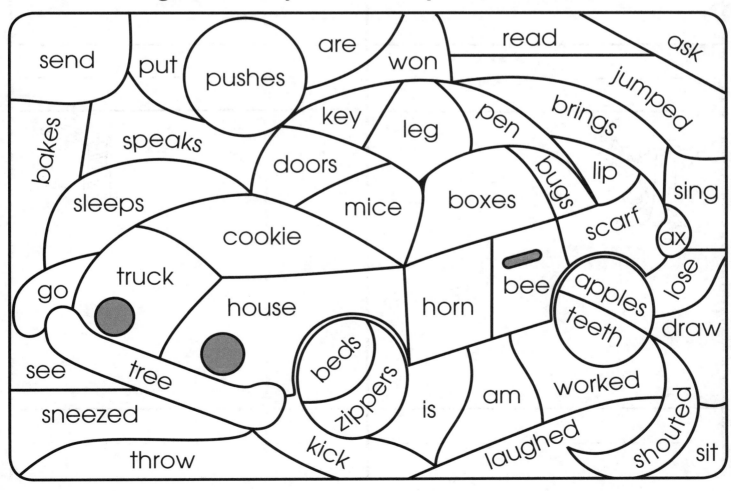

Write the **verbs** in the boxes.
Draw pictures to show what is happening.

run home play jump throw big

Name _____ Date _____

read

Circle the **verb** in each sentence.
Cut out the sentence strips.
Paste them under the correct pictures.

A

B

C

D

E

F

Run fast.

Hit the ball.

Throw it to me.

Sit on it.

Jump rope.

Slide down.

Find the **verb** to go with each subject.
Write the word on the line.
Draw a picture that shows all the things in the story.

1. I – – – – – little.

_____

_____

2. My legs – – – – – – short.

_____

_____

3. My shell – – – – – – – my house.

_____

_____

4. My colors – – – – – – green and brown.

_____

_____

5. I – – – – – – – able to swim.

_____

_____

6. A funny hat – – – – – – on my head.

_____

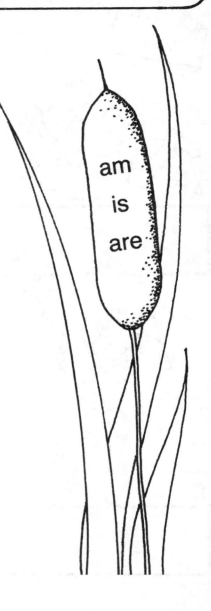

am
is
are

Circle the sentence
that does not belong
with the rest.

A **verb** is a word that shows action.

Circle the verb in each sentence.
Use those verbs to fill in the puzzle.

Across

2. The cougar leaps from the ledge.
5. A squirrel climbs the tree.
7. A deer jumps the fence.
8. The kittens play with the vine.
9. Birds fly.

Down

1. The raccoon washes his food.
3. The owl swoops down to the ground.
4. The puppies dig a hole.
5. Turtles crawl on a log.
6. The fish swim in the lake.

Name _____   Date _____

Polly's pointers:

A word that shows action is a **verb**. When a verb tells what one person or thing is doing now, it usually ends with the letter **s**, unless the subject of the sentence is **you** or **I**.

Examples: Boris **speaks**. You **speak**.
The man **paints**. I **paint**.

Circle the correct word in the parentheses below.

Dorothy (sing, sings) very sweetly. Her twin brothers (play, plays) the piano well. Dorothy's father (direct, directs) the orchestra. What a musical family!

Children (enjoy, enjoys) Mrs. Winkler's class. Sometimes they (cut, cuts) oval shapes from paper. They (paint, paints) faces on them. Then the boys and girls (glue, glues) yarn on the oval for hair. Mrs. Winkler (smile, smiles) at the children's pictures. She (say, says) that they do nice art work.

Polly's pointer:

The **present tense** of a verb tells about something happening now, something that happens regularly, or something that is about to happen.

Examples: I **paint**. I **paint** every day. I **paint** this evening.

Write a predicate for each subject, using an action verb in the **present tense**.

1. The busy little bees _____ .

2. My cousin John _____ .

3. Most third graders _____ .

4. Suddenly, Mr. Boyd _____ .

5. The giant panda bear _____ .

Write a sentence about something that is happening right now.

Name _____ Date _____

Circle the **verb** that agrees with each subject.
Write the verb on the line in the sentence.

1. go
   went

2. are
   were

3. is
   was

4. see
   saw

5. are
   were

6. see
   saw

_____

1. Rosita – – – – – – – – – – to the pond.

_____

2. Yesterday the fish – – – – – – – – – not there.

_____

3. Only the frog – – – – – – – – – – there then.

_____

4. Later she – – – – – – – – – – the fish.

_____

5. They – – – – – – – – – – back in the pond.

_____

6. What will Rosita – – – – – – – – – next?

_____

Find the correct **verb** to go in each sentence.
Write it on the line.
Color the space for that word in the puzzle.

_____

1. Butterflies – – – – – – – with their feelers.

_____

2. They always – – – – – – – – – in the daytime.

_____

3. The yellow butterfly – – – – – – – – – – – the flowers.

_____

4. It – – – – – – – – – – – to go from flower to flower.

_____

5. The brown butterfly – – – – – – – – – – – – – the yellow one.

_____

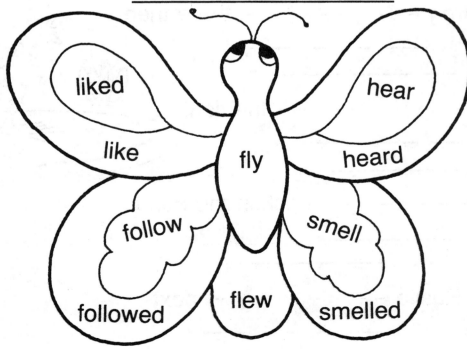

Find the correct **verb** to go in each sentence.
Write it on the line.

1. The little bee always – – – – – – – –very hard.

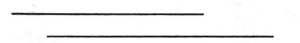

2. Yesterday the bee – – – – – – – – – – all day.

works
worked

3. I heard the bee as he – – – – – – – – – – –by.

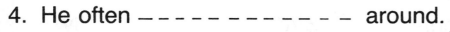

4. He often – – – – – – – – – – – – around.

buzzes
buzzed

5. Bees – – – – – – – – –very fast.

6. Three bees – – – – – – – – –past me.

fly
flew

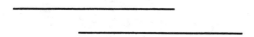

7. The bees – – – – – – – – – some honey.

make
made

8. We can – – – – – – – – – –a sandwich with it.

Draw a line to match each sentence with the correct **verb.**
Circle the sentence that tells about the picture.

1. The boy ____.   walks
   The boys ____.   walk

2. A rabbit ____.   hop
   Rabbits ____.   hops

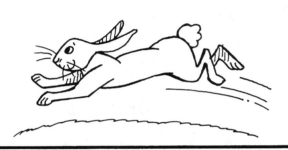

3. A snake ____.   wiggles
   Snakes ____.   wiggle

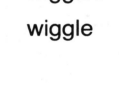

4. A bird ____.   flies
   Birds ____.   fly

5. A horse ____.   trot
   Horses ____.   trots

6. A dog ____.   barks
   Dogs ____.   bark

A **verb** can tell about something that has already happened.
This is often done by adding **ed** to the verb.
<u>Example</u>: help ——→ help**ed**
Today, I **help**.
Yesterday, I **helped**.

Complete each box below.

Today	Yesterday
pull	
	cooked
laugh	
play	
	opened
	jumped
wash	
talk	

Today	Yesterday
	finished
look	
listen	
	barked
paint	
	walked
	fixed
fish	

Write the correct word in each blank.

1. Each day, I _____ to the playground.
   walk   walked

2. Yesterday, we _____ to a story.
   listen   listened

3. Last week, the boys _____ hockey.
   play   played

Write a sentence about the dinner you had last night.

Name _____ Date _____

Irregular verbs
change in spelling when they tell about something that has already happened.

In each pair of verbs below, one shows a change in spelling. It tells about something that has already happened. Write the correct form of each of these **irregular verbs** on the lines below.

_____

1. The sign _____ down a week ago.
   fall   fell
   _____

2. Kevin _____ on his hat Tuesday.
   sat   sit
   _____

3. Yesterday, Adam _____ a bear.
   see   saw
   _____

4. They _____ lunch with me last week.
   ate   eat
   _____

5. The other day, Gina _____ a mile.
   run   ran
   _____

6. Carlos _____ four inches last year.
   grew   grow
   _____

7. Last week, they _____ sick.
   get   got

EXTRA! Write a sentence about something that happened yesterday.
Did you use an irregular verb?

Name _____ Date _____

Use **does** and **do** to tell about now.
Use **does** to tell about one, but not with you or I.
Use **do** to tell about more than one and with you and I.
Use **did** to tell about something that has already happened.

Write the correct word in each blank. Use **does** or **do**.

1. Charlotte _____ not have a bike.

2. You _____ the dishes today.

3. They _____ not need any help.

4. Gary _____ a lot of work.

5. The boys _____ many different things.

Make each sentence tell about something that happened in the past by changing **does** or **do** to **did**.

1. You do not know her name.

_____

_____

2. Michael does all of the painting.

_____

_____

Use **has** and **have** to tell about now.
Use **has** to tell about one, but not with you or I.
Use **have** to tell about more than
one and always with you and I.
Use **had** to tell about something that
has already happened.

Underline the correct word in ( ) in each sentence.

1. You (has, have) to take a test.

2. We (has, have) to wash the dishes.

3. Eric (has, have) on my coat.

4. Luis (has, have) a new soccer ball.

5. I (has, have) an ice cream cone.

6. They (has, have) found the lost dog.

Change each sentence so that it tells about something that has already happened by changing **have** or **has** to **had**.

1. He has a broken arm.

_____

- -

_____

2. I have seven crayons.

_____

- -

_____

Use **was** and **were** to tell about the past.
Use **was** to tell about one.
Use **were** to tell about more than one.
Use **were** with you.

Write the correct word in each blank. Use **was** or **were**.

1. We _____ having a picnic.

2. Sara _____ the first one there.

3. The cars _____ stopping.

4. Andy _____ here yesterday.

5. I _____ in the first row.

6. They _____ at the party.

Cross out the word that would NOT follow the words given.

| he (was, were) | the teachers (was, were) |
| my mother (was, were) | Travis Price (was, were) |

Finish the four sentences above.

Use **is** to tell about one person or thing, but never with you or I.
Use **are** to tell about more than one person or thing.
Always use **am** with the word I.
Always use **are** with the word you.

Fill each blank by using is, are, or am.

1. Jacob _____ ten years old.

2. The girls _____ going for a hike.

3. I _____ four feet tall.

4. Andrea _____ going to the store.

5. They _____ in the red car.

6. Joan _____ my best friend.

Draw a line to match the beginning of each sentence
with the word that would follow it.

He	are	I	is	Sue	am
We	is	She	are	I	are
I	am	They	am	You	is

Use **a** when a word begins with a consonant sound.
Use **an** when a word begins with a vowel sound.

Write *a* or *an* in each sentence.

1. The Chens visited _____ aquarium.

2. They saw _____ octopus with eight arms.

3. Dolphins ate fish from _____ woman's hand.

4. _____ diver fed fish in a big tank.

5. _____ eel was long and snakelike.

6. A man rode on the back of _____ whale.

7. Mrs. Chen took pictures with _____ camera.

Write *a* or *an* in each blank.

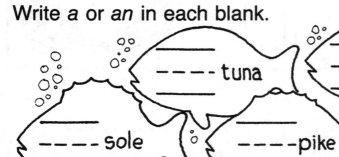 _____ tuna

_____ catfish

_____ oyster

_____ sole

_____ pike

_____ anchovy

_____ angelfish

The words **a** and **an** are used before a noun that names one person, place, or thing.

Use **an** before a noun that begins with a vowel.

Use **a** before a noun that begins with a consonant.

Write **a** or **an** in each blank.

_____ goose	_____ book	_____ door
_____ baby	_____ horse	_____ ruler
_____ owl	_____ apple	_____ umbrella
_____ animal	_____ ant	_____ snake

Draw a line from the correct word to the picture.

a an	a an	a an
a an	a an	a an

Make a list of three things to buy at the store. Be sure to use **a** or **an**.

Read each pair of sentences.
Think about what the underlined word in the second sentence means.
Circle the word or words it tells about in the first sentence.

1. Ben is a brown bear.
   He can ride a bike.

2. The bike is very nice.
   It is bright red.

3. There is a horn on the bike.
   I think it is loud.

4. Jan is a bear, too.
   She wants a bike like Ben's.

5. Ben and Jan can both ride.
   They do tricks on the bikes.

6. The bears are in a circus.
   They like it there.

Draw a picture of Ben and Jan on the bike.

What else is happening in Ben and Jan's circus? Add other circus acts to your drawing.

Read the sentences in each box.
Think about what the underlined word means.
Circle the word or words it tells about.
Draw a picture of the words you circle.

1. Mary, Bob, and I will go to the park. <u>We</u> can play there.	2. The slide is big. We can go down <u>it</u>.
3. Mary likes the swings best. <u>They</u> go up high.	4. Bob wants to play ball. <u>He</u> is a good player.
5. I like to go with Mary. <u>She</u> always plays with me.	6. The park is very big. <u>It</u> has a lot of things.

Name _____   Date _____

Always write **I** with a capital letter.
Always name yourself last.
Use **I** in the subject part of a sentence.
Use **me** in the predicate part.

Complete each sentence with **I** or **me**.

_____

1. Sarah and _____ helped Mom.

_____

2. _____ made my bed.

_____

3. Sarah and_____ picked up our toys.

_____

4. Mom gave _____ a bowl.

_____

5. _____ fed the dog.

_____

6. Sarah helped _____ carry the trash.

_____

7. _____ thanked Sarah for the help.

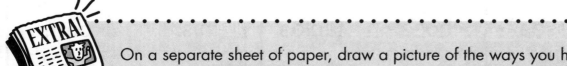

On a separate sheet of paper, draw a picture of the ways you help out at home.

> Use **this** and **that** with nouns
> that name only one thing.
>
> Use **these** and **those** with nouns
> that name more than one thing.

Underline the word in ( ) that fits in each sentence.

1. (These, This) is not your .

2. Are (these, that) your 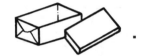 ?

3. (That, These) is Renee's  .

4. (This, Those) are my 📚 .

5. Put your 👟 into (that, these) 📦 .

6. I saw (that, those) 🧱 fall.

A sentence with a picture in place of a word is called a **rebus**.
On another sheet of paper, make your own rebus sentences.

Draw lines to connect the words that go together.

this	books	those	bears	this	birds
those	book	that	bear	these	bird
that	dress	that	table	these	pen
these	dresses	those	tables	this	pens

A word made from two words is a **compound**.

Draw lines between the words to make compounds. Write each compound in the correct sentence.

fire	cake
pan	fire
camp	wood

table	berries
out	doors
blue	spoon

_____

1. The scouts picked up _____ .

2. They built a _____ .

3. Some scouts made _____ batter.

4. They mixed the batter with a _____ .

5. They added _____ to the mix.

6. It was fun to eat _____ .

Cross out letters in the two words to make a **contraction.** Write the contraction with an ' in the place of the missing letters.

1. I will	2. He is
_ _ _ _ _ _ _ _ _ _	_ _ _ _ _ _ _ _ _ _
3. she would	4. we are
_ _ _ _ _ _ _ _ _ _	_ _ _ _ _ _ _ _ _ _
5. do not	6. they will
_ _ _ _ _ _ _ _ _ _	_ _ _ _ _ _ _ _ _ _

EXTRA! Write a sentence using one of the contractions you made above.

A **contraction** is a short way of writing two words.
An **apostrophe** (') takes the place of letters that have been left out.

Draw a line to match the words with their contractions.

is not	aren't	we are	she's	I will	he'll
does not	isn't	I am	he's	he will	I'll
are not	doesn't	she is	we're	they will	we'll
has not	won't	they are	I'm	we will	they'll
will not	hasn't	he is	they're	she will	she'll

Write contractions for the words in ( ). Complete the sentences.

1. It (is not) _____ time for the race to start.

2. (They are) _____ marking lines on the field.

3. (They will) _____ blow a whistle to start the race.

4. I hope it (does not) _____ rain today.

Use a contraction from the box to write a sentence telling how the race ends.

An **adjective** is a word that describes a noun. Any word that completes this sentence is an **adjective**:

It is very _____ .

Circle each word below that fits in the sentence above.

dark	laugh	dog	cold	boy
red	window	good	soft	wet
big	old	bike	orange	hard

Choose three **adjectives** from the box to describe each noun below. Cross out each word as you use it.

wet	white	hot
cold	yellow	gray
soft	small	big

mouse _____   _____   _____

snow _____   _____   _____

sun _____   _____   _____

Color words are used to describe things.
Color words are **adjectives**.

Choose one **color word** to complete each sentence below.

1. I see the _____ sun.

2. The grass is very _____ .

3. The _____ sky is very pretty.

4. _____ snow is all around us.

5. Glenn ate the _____ grapes.

6. David saw the _____ stop sign.

7. The pumpkin was _____ .

8. At night, the sky looks very _____ .

pink

purple

orange

brown

red

white

black

green

yellow

blue

EXTRA!

Fill in each oval in the color word list with the correct color crayon.

> **Remember:** An **adjective** is
> a describing word.

Underline the **adjective** in each pair of words.

1. egg, easy

2. fat, fall

3. yellow, yawn

4. fast, fudge

5. cold, cupcake

6. flower, flat

7. toe, tall

8. house, huge

9. loud, lamp

10. button, big

11. fuzzy, farm

12. rock, round

Write each **adjective** below the picture it best describes.

hard	cold
round	sharp
hot	soft

_____

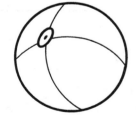

Some things
can be described by more
than one **adjective**.

Read the **adjectives** in each box.
Color the picture that they both describe.

fuzzy and old	cold and large
sharp and tiny	furry and small
sweet and soft	hot and big

Name _____ Date _____

Add **er** to the words in ( ).

_____

- - - - - - - - - - - - -

1. A turtle is (slow) _____ than a fox.

_____

- - - - - - - - - - - - -

2. A bass is (short) _____ than a swordfish.

Add **est** to the words in ( ).

_____

- - - - - - - - - - - - -

3. The giraffe is the (tall) _____ of all animals.

_____

- - - - - - - - - - - - -

4. The python is one of the (long) _____ snakes.

Add **er** or **est** to the words in ( ).

_____

- - - - - - - - - - - - -

5. A zebra is (fast) _____ than a rhino.

_____

- - - - - - - - - - - - -

6. The cheetah is (fast) _____ of all.

_____

- - - - - - - - - - - - -

7. A mountain lion is (small) _____ than a tiger.

EXTRA! Write a sentence comparing students to teachers.

A **synonym** is a word that has the same or almost the same meaning as another word.

Look at the words in ( ) in each sentence. Find a synonym.
Cut and paste it on the blank.

1. Sue and Betsy (run) _____ every day.

2. They follow a (path) _____ in the park.

3. The trail goes through the (woods) _____.

4. A bridge crosses a (stream) _____.

5. Betsy's (hat) _____ flew off her head.

6. The girls (laughed) _____ at the bobbing hat.

brook	trail	cap
forest	giggled	jog

Antonyms are words with **opposite meanings.**

Find an antonym for each word in ( ). Write the word on the dotted line.
Use the word bank.

dark	south	thick
long	stayed	Winter

1. Barney Bear's fur was getting (thin) _____.

2. Many birds were flying (north) _____.

3. (Summer) _____ was coming.

4. Barney was ready for a (short) __ __ __ nap.

5. He found a (light) __ __ __ cave.

6. Barney Bear (left) __ __ __ __ __ and slept.

How did Barney feel when he woke up?
Write the circled letters in order on these lines.

___ ___ ___ ___ ___ ___

___ ___ ___ ___ ___ ___

___ ___ ___ ___ ___ ___
1   2   3   4   5   6

Some words sound the same but have different spellings and meanings.

Write the correct word in each sentence.

_____

_ _ _ _ _

1. We walk _____ school. (to, two)

_____

_ _ _ _ _ _ _ _

2. We turn _____ at the corner. (write, right)

_____

_ _ _ _ _ _ _ _

3. The crossing guard will _____ us. (meat, meet)

_____

_ _ _ _ _ _ _

4. We stop when the light turns _____ . (red, read)

Play tic-tac-toe. Find three words in each box that sound the same but
have different spellings and meanings. Color the three spaces yellow. The
words can go across (⟶), down (↓), or at an angle (↘).

to	rode	road
see	two	wood
sea	would	too

won	know	no
one	son	sun
there	their	they're

hear	here	so
blue	ate	sew
blew	eight	sow

Write the rhyming words in the poem.

| log | frog | dog | my | fly | | glad | sad | bad | run | fun |
|-----|------|-----|-----|-----| |------|-----|-----|-----|-----|

There once was a little green

_ _ _ _ _ _ _ _ _ _ _ _ _ _ _ _

_____,

Who sat in the sun on a

_ _ _ _ _ _ _ _ _ _ _ _ _ _ _ _

_____.

He ate a big

_ _ _ _ _ _ _ _ _ _ _ _ _ _ _ _

_____

And then said, "Oh

_ _ _ _ _ _ _ _ _ _ _ _ _ _ _ _

_____,

I'm glad that I'm not a

_____,"

_ _ _ _ _ _ _ _ _ _ _ _ _ _ _ _

_____.

The dog said to him, "That's too

_ _ _ _ _ _ _ _ _ _ _ _ _ _ _ _

_____.

If you were a dog I'd be

_ _ _ _ _ _ _ _ _ _ _ _ _ _ _ _

_____

We could have lots of

_ _ _ _ _ _ _ _ _ _ _ _ _ _ _ _

_____.

We could bark and

_ _ _ _ _ _ _ _ _ _ _ _ _ _ _ _

_____,

And then I would not be so

_____,"

_ _ _ _ _ _ _ _ _ _ _ _ _ _ _ _

On a separate sheet of paper, draw a picture about the poem.

Underline the rhyming words in the poem.
Write the rhyming words on the lines.

I would like to ride a train
Or a bus, or a big jet plane;

Maybe I'd go in a car
To a place that's not so far;

Or perhaps I'd run or skate
To a town across the state;

But no matter where I go
I'm always fast—not slow.

Name _____   Date _____

A **simple sentence** can
be made with one **noun** followed
by one **verb**.

Choose a **noun** and a **verb** to make a **simple sentence**. Write each sentence on the lines below.

Noun

birds
rabbits
people
babies
lions

Verb

hop
crawl
roar
fly
talk

1. _____

2. _____

3. _____

4. _____

5. _____

Look out the window. Write a simple sentence about something that you see.

Who or what a sentence is about is called the **subject**. The **subject** of a sentence always includes a noun.

Example: Joe sails boats.
         Joe and Lee sail boats.

Underline the word or group of words that tells who or what did the action in each sentence. This is the **subject** of the sentence.

Dale sings a song.	Her friend waved.
Ted went fishing.	A bird can fly.
The balloon blew away.	The girls ate breakfast.
Five cats ran past me.	Babies cannot walk.
The bike is green.	His father plays baseball.
Curtis fell down.	Belinda and Jan got lost.

Circle each word or group of words that can be used as a **subject**.

Jimmy	ate lunch	the park
fell down	Aunt Rita	read a book
my sister	cut his hair	my pencil

EXTRA!

Choose one of the sentences above and draw a picture of its subject.

Name _____ Date _____

Find the **subject** that goes in each sentence.
Write the word on the line.
Cut and paste the picture in the box.

1. _____

   _ _ _ _ _ _ _

   The _____ leaks.

2. _____

   _ _ _ _ _ _ _

   The _____ leak.

3. _____

   _ _ _ _ _ _ _

   The red _____ bounce.

4. _____

   _ _ _ _ _ _ _

   The blue _____ bounces.

5. _____

   _ _ _ _ _ _ _

   Big _____ fly best.

6. _____

   _ _ _ _ _ _ _

   A little _____ flies high.

cup   cups    kite

kites    balls 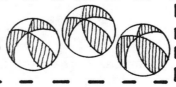   ball

Name _____   Date _____

A sentence is made up of a naming part and an action part. The naming part is called the **subject**. The subject tells who or what the sentence is about.

Find the subject for each sentence.
Cut and paste it on the blank.

1. _____ blows a horn.

2. _____ rolls a ball.

3. _____ jumps through a hoop.

4. _____ trot around the ring.

5. _____ sells popcorn.

6. _____ ride in a car.

| Two clowns | A man | Three horses |
| A tiger | An elephant | A seal |

The part of a sentence that tells what the
subject is doing or did is called the **predicate**.
The **predicate** shows action and always has a verb.

Match each **subject** with a **predicate**.

Subject	Predicate
The team	rolled away.
My bike	blew away from her.
A baby	baked a cake.
The cook	won the game.
The kite	dropped its bottle.

Circle each group of words that can be used as a **predicate**.

the airplane	builds a table	a doctor
writes a letter	the woman	jumped over it
sings very loudly	Jeanne	the snowman
my mother	ran away	ate a carrot

Write two complete sentences using the groups of words above.

54

The **subject** tells who or what the sentence is about.
The **predicate** tells what the subject is doing or did.

Write **S** next to each word or group of words that can be used as a **subject**. Write **P** next to each word or group of words that can be used as a **predicate**.

was wet _____	the sun _____	flew away _____
Sue's coat _____	the boat _____	were sad _____
eat lunch _____	sailed away _____	went upstairs _____
saw a dog _____	my sister _____	the birds _____
is warm _____	Paul _____	the dishes _____

Choose subjects and predicates from the list above to make three good sentences. Remember to use capital letters and periods.

_____

_____

_____

_____

_____

_____

Two sentences can have the
same words but different **meaning**. Changing the order
of words can change the meaning.

Draw a line from each sentence to the correct picture.

The boy hit the ball.

The ball hit the boy.

The mouse scared the cat.

The cat scared the mouse.

The hat was on the horse.

The horse was on the hat.

The seal ate a fish.

A fish ate the seal.

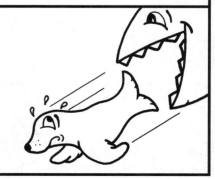

Find the **right order** for the words to make a sentence.
Connect the dots in that order.
Write the sentence.

make

can ———————— a

I house

———————————————————————

This

big truck

is

———————————————————————

little The

is box

———————————————————————

I here

can eat

———————————————————————

The words in a **sentence** must be in an order that makes sense.

Make sentences by putting each group of words in the correct order.

1. balloon. The had a red girl

_____

_____

2. Pelicans eat to fish. like

_____

_____

3. read She books this month. five

_____

_____

4. a cat. Eric has black

_____

_____

5. in the ball went goal. The

_____

_____

Draw one line under the subject and two lines under the predicate of each sentence.

Write the words in the **right order** to make a sentence.
Start with a **capital letter**. End with a **period**.

mix   get   cake   a

_____

- -

_____

it   mix

_____

- -

_____

the   bake   cake

_____

- -

_____

cake   the   eat

_____

- -

_____

A sentence must make sense.
The words in a sentence must be in **order**.

1.

2.

3.

4.

5.

Change the words around to make sense.
Cut and paste one sentence at a time.

1.	go	library.	to	the	We

2.	read	books.	We

3.	records.	to	listen	We

4.	have	card.	I	library	a

5.	May	borrow	books?	I	some

Changing the **word order** in a sentence can change its meaning.

Draw a line from each sentence to the correct picture.

	The dog scared the cat. The cat scared the dog.	
	The goat followed the boy. The boy followed the goat.	
	A clown laughed at a girl. A girl laughed at a clown.	

The sentences below are questions.
Write the same words in a different order to answer the questions.

1. Can Mark fix it?

   _____

   _____

   _____

2. Is Rudy here?

   _____

   _____

   _____

Circle the subject in each of the above sentences.

The words in a sentence must be in order.

Read the words on each ball. Write the words in sentence order.
Remember to start with a capital letter and to end with a period.

play
we
soccer

_____

_____

field
is
long
the

_____

_____

Heidi
the
ball
kicks

_____

_____

our
scores
team

_____

_____

Draw one line under the subject of each sentence.
Draw two lines under each predicate.

A **sentence** is a group of words that makes sense.
Remember: A **sentence** ends with a period.

Color each space blue if it contains a complete **sentence**.
Color the other spaces orange.
Put a period after each complete sentence.

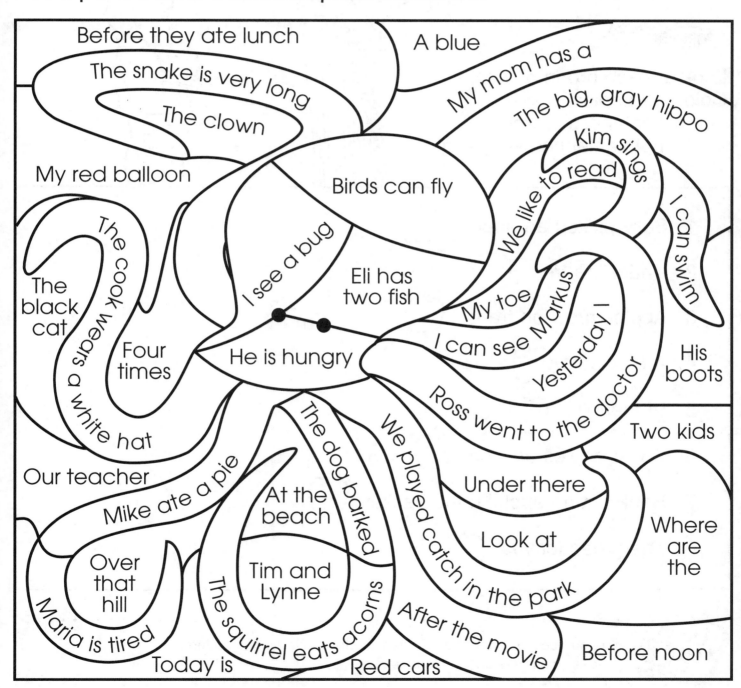

A **sentence** is a group of words that tells a whole idea.

Look at each group of words.
Color the apples.

    sentences — red
    not sentences — green

1. Sally picked an apple.

2. Under the tree

3. Apples grow on trees.

4. Are sweet

5. In the fall

6. Some apples are red.

7. Hank put an apple in the basket.

8. The green leaves

EXTRA!

The numbers in front of the sentences are hidden in the picture.
Find the numbers and circle them.

A sentence tells a whole idea.

Find the sentences. Write them.

1. a. We had a fire drill.   b. A fire drill

- -

_____

2. a. The bell rang.   b. The loud bell

- -

_____

3. a. Our class   b. Our class lined up.

- -

_____

4. a. On the outside   b. We walked outside.

- -

_____

5. a. The school was empty.   b. The school

- -

_____

Write a sentence about the last time your school had a fire drill.

Underline each **complete sentence**.

good

it is good

like it

i like it

it is big

i will get it

Write the complete sentences that were underlined.
Start with a capital letter.
End with a period.

_____

_____

_____

_____

_____

_____

_____

Find the **complete sentences**.
Circle the first letter of each sentence.
Write the **capital letter** above it.
Put a **period** at the end of each sentence.

here it is

so good

it is for you

you can eat it

i like

this is for me

too much

i am full

EXTRA!

Color the scoops of ice cream that have complete sentences.

Use the word **and** to combine the sentences. Write the new sentence on the lines.

Example: I like cereal. I like milk.
I like cereal and milk.

1.   I like dogs.   I like cats.

_____

_____

_____

2.   We have candy.   We have gum.

_____

_____

_____

3.   I will eat ham.   I will eat eggs.

_____

_____

_____

Some **sentences** can be **combined.**
Use **and** to join the parts.

and

In each pair of sentences, combine the subjects with **and.**
Write the combined sentence.

1. My hands are cold.
   My feet are cold.

   _____

   _____

2. Anna can bake pies.
   Michael can bake pies.

   _____

   _____

3. Cows are in the barn.
   Horses are in the barn.

   _____

   _____

In each pair of sentences, combine the predicates with **and.**
Write the combined sentence.

4. The dog barked.
   The dog growled.

   _____

   _____

5. Jenny can hop.
   Jenny can skip.

   _____

   _____

Think of two things you like to do after school. Write one sentence about these things using **and.**

A **statement** is a sentence that **tells** something.
A **question** is a sentence that **asks** something.
A **command** is a sentence that **gives an order**.
An **exclamation** is a sentence that **shows strong feeling**.

Color:

statements—red   commands—green
questions—blue   exclamations—orange

I went fishing.

The wagon is red.

She fed the kitten.

Hank paints a picture.

Who is first?

Did he find it?

Is lunch ready?

Where is my shirt?

Look out!

It's falling!

It burned my hand!

The lion is loose!

Put it here.

Close the door.

Open your book.

Wash your hands.

EXTRA!

At the top of each umbrella section, draw the punctuation mark used at the end of each sentence type.

A sentence that tells something is called a **statement**. A statement begins with a capital letter. It ends with a period.

Frog

Toad

Write each statement correctly.

1. a frog is smooth and shiny

_____

_____

2. it has long legs

_____

_____

3. frogs lay eggs in clumps

_____

_____

4. the toad has rough skin

_____

_____

5. it has short legs

_____

_____

On another sheet of paper, rearrange the words in each statement to ask a question.

A **statement** tells something.
A **question** asks something.
A **statement** can be turned into a **question** by changing the word order.
Example: This is a dog.
Is this a dog?

Change each **statement** to a **question**. Use the same words, but change the order. Add a question mark. Look at the pictures and circle the correct answer to each **question**.

1. I can ride on this.

_____

_____

yes   no

2. The monkey is eating.

_____

_____

yes   no

3. This is a bicycle.

_____

_____

yes   no

4. The boy is running.

_____

_____

yes   no

For all of the questions that you circled "no," draw a picture of a correct answer.

A **wh** question asks for information. **Wh** questions begin with: **Who**, **What**, **When**, **Where**, or **Why**.

Match each **wh** word with the rest of its question.

Who	are you sad?
What	do you live?
When	is your teacher?
Where	is your birthday?
Why	is your name?

Write **who**, **what**, **when**, or **where** after each group of words to tell which question it answers.

the house _____

in the car _____

by the library _____

Victor _____

his sister_____

my slippers _____

at two o'clock _____

next week _____

Answer each of the questions at the top of the page with a complete sentence.

Cut out the sentence strips.
Paste them in the boxes in the correct order to tell a story.
Draw a picture in each box to show what is happening.

1

2

3

4

A
I will put butter on it.

C
I will get popcorn and a pan.

B
I will pop the popcorn.

D
Then I will eat it.

Name _____   Date _____

Cut and paste the sentences under the correct **topic sentence.**
Draw a picture to go with each story.

1. We learn a lot of things in school.

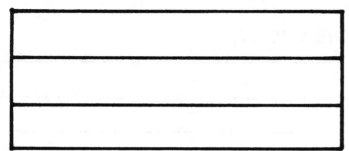

2. I know how to make things.

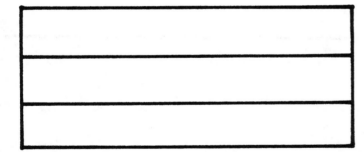

We learn to read.	I can make a picture.
I can make a kite.	We learn to add numbers.
We learn to sing.	I can make cookies.

Read the story.
Choose the **topic sentence** that tells the main idea of the story. Write it on the lines.

We will take food in a basket.
We will go to the park.
Then we can play games and eat.

_____

- -

_____

- -

_____

Topic sentences:
1. Dad and I have work to do.
2. It is time to go to school.
3. Today we will go on a picnic.

Draw a picture of the story.

Find a book or story you have read. Choose a paragraph and write down its topic sentence.

A **topic sentence** tells the **main idea** of a **paragraph**.
A topic sentence tells what all the sentences in the paragraph are about.

Read the sentences. Choose the correct topic sentence for each paragraph. Write the topic sentence on the line.

Topic
sentences:

We had a Halloween party.
Sound travels in waves.
Our class made salt dough.

_____

_ _

_____

When something moves, it makes the air around it move. The waves are pushed on and on. When the waves reach our ears, we hear them as sounds.

_____

_ _

_____

First, we put salt, water, and cornstarch into a pan. Then we cooked it for five minutes. Finally, we squeezed it with our hands.

_____

_ _

_____

Mrs. Harris planned the games. Some mothers brought treats. Everyone wore a costume.

Indent the first word in a paragraph. That means to move it a little to the right. The other sentences in the paragraph are not indented.

Write these sentences in paragraph form. Indent the first word.

The pelican has a special pouch in its bill.
The pouch can hold water.
The pelican uses it as a scoop to catch fish.

Write a story that tells what is happening in each picture.

boy sticks paper string kite flew down

On another sheet of paper, draw a picture of a scene from your favorite story.

A **paragraph** is a group of sentences that tell about **one main idea.**

Read the paragraph below. Find the sentence that does not belong. Draw a line through it. Copy the other sentences to make a paragraph.

Felicia likes to bring her lunch to school. She can pack her favorite foods. Whales are larger than elephants. She doesn't have to stand in line for a tray.

A letter has five parts: the **date**, the **greeting**, the **body,** the **closing,** and the **signature.**

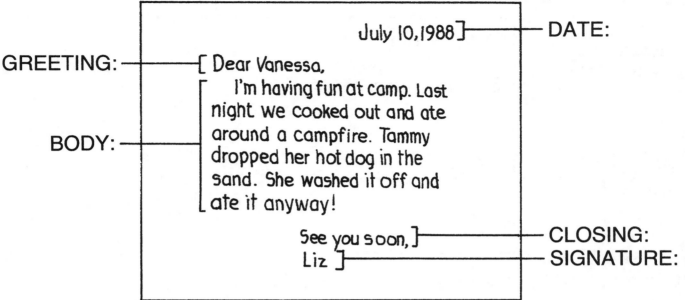

July 10, 1988 — DATE:

GREETING: — Dear Vanessa,

BODY: — I'm having fun at camp. Last night we cooked out and ate around a campfire. Tammy dropped her hot dog in the sand. She washed it off and ate it anyway!

See you soon, — CLOSING:
Liz — SIGNATURE:

Here is a letter that Val wrote.
Circle:

the date in blue.   the body in yellow.
the greeting in red.   the closing in green.
         the signature in orange.

March 25, 1989

Dear Kim,
    We moved into our new house on Friday. I have my own bedroom. Mom says I have to keep it clean. Guess I'll have to learn to hang up my clothes and keep Scruffy off the bed.

        Your friend,
        Val

An **envelope** has two parts.
The **mailing address** tells who will **receive** the letter.
The **return address** tells who is **sending** the letter.

RETURN
ADDRESS

Dave Santel
26 Thicket Lane
Dallas, Texas 75252

MAILING
ADDRESS

Mr. Paul Kinder
211 Florence Place
Clearwater, Florida 34623

Use these addresses to address the envelope correctly.

Return address:
    Jim Conley
    304 Wexler Lane
    Tempe, Arizona 85282

Mailing address:
    Alma Scott
    7 Mardel Avenue
    Union, Missouri 63084

When you fill out a form, remember:
1. Read each line carefully.
2. Write neatly on each line.
3. Check your work.

Fill out these forms.

ENTRY FORM
GREEN PARK RUN

Name

Age

School

Grade

LIBRARY CARD

City Library

Name

Grade

Teacher's Name

Name _____ Date _____

One way to list words is in **alphabetical order.** When words begin with the same first letter, you must look at the second letter in each word.

Sam says his friends can take turns on his skateboard. List the friends' names in alphabetical order.

Kurt

Althea

Art

Manuel

Kenny

Karen

Cora

Larry

1. _____   5. _____

2. _____   6. _____

3. _____   7. _____

4. _____   8. _____

Put these words in alphabetical order to make sentences. Remember capital letters and periods. Can you do what the first sentence tells you to do?

1. this twister say tongue

_____

_____

2. sells skateboards Sam

_____

_____

Write the words in **ABC order.**
Connect the dots.
Start with the first word in ABC order.

house
•

• fun   jump •

• dog   pet •

bark   wag

Choose two of the words to make a compound word that tells about the picture.

Write the words in **ABC order** to make sentences. Draw a picture to go with the story.

flew   bird   the   window.   A   in

- -

- -

table.   It   red   Pat's   on   landed

- -

- -

EXTRA! Write a sentence telling what happens next in the story.

Write the names of the **holidays** in ABC order.
Start each name with a **capital letter.**
Draw a line from dot to dot in ABC order.

• christmas

labor day •

fourth
of july •

easter •

• thanksgiving

1. _____

2. _____

3. _____

4. _____

5. _____

Help the monkey get to the zoo.
Write the names of the streets in ABC order.
Start each **street name** with a **capital letter.**

funny road

zoo street

ape avenue

happy drive

lucky street

big road

dandy drive

1. _____

2. _____

3. _____

4. _____

5. _____

6. _____

7. _____

EXTRA!

Draw the monkey at the zoo.

Circle the **name** of a **person** in each sentence.
Write the name under the correct picture.
Start each name with a **capital letter**.

1. mike has a hat.

2. candy has a bow.

3. ken has a ball.

4. pam has long hair.

5. beth has a doll.

6. matt has a bell.

89

Write the names of people and pets.
Start each name with a **capital letter**.
An initial is always a **capital letter**.

joe l. brown

t. j. jones

i. m. good

ann crow

champ   puff

90

The names of people and pets begin with **capital letters**.

Write the correct name for each person and pet.

beth bandit	juan boots	polly tony
harvey jared	buster kim	debbie fluffy
smoky ruby	gretchen denny	lois duchess

Titles for people begin with capital letters.
Most titles end with a period.
Miss does not end with a period.
An **initial** is always a capital letter.
End an initial with a period.

Write the titles and initials correctly on the name tags.

mr wong	mr J P ross
miss perez	dr c clark
dr hollis	miss r bell

Pretend it is the first day of school. Draw your own nametag with your correct title.

Write each sentence.
Use capital **I** when it is a word by itself.

1. See what i am.

_____

- -

_____

2. i can swim.

_____

- -

_____

3. i can walk.

_____

- -

_____

4. i can quack.

_____

- -

_____

5. What am i?

_____

- -

_____

Draw a picture of me.

Write the days of the week in order.
Start each one with a **capital letter**.

wednesday   friday   saturday   monday
sunday   tuesday   thursday

_____
1. I like _ .
_____
_____

2. On _ we go to school.
_____

3. Next _ _ _ _ _ _ _ _ _ _ _ _ _ _ _ _ _ _ _ I will play ball.
_____

4. _ may be sunny.

_____
_____

5. _ may be rainy.
_____

6. On _ I will see Bob.

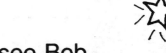

_____

7. I can see TV on _ _ _ _ _ _ _ _ _ _ _ _ _ _ _ _ _ .
_____

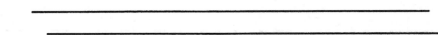

Write the names of the **months**.
Start each name with a **capital letter**.

january

february

march

april

may

june

july

august

september

october

november

december

Write the sentences on the lines.
Start the name of each **month** with a **capital letter**.
Draw a picture about each sentence.

1. It snows in january.

2. We swim in july.

3. I can fly a kite in march.

4. We go to school in september.

The names of **days, months,** and **holidays** begin with capital letters.

| Sunday | Monday | Tuesday | Wednesday | Thursday | Friday | Saturday |

Complete the sentences.

1. The first day of the week is _____ .

2. The day after Wednesday is _____ .

3. _____ is the day before Saturday.

| January | March | May | July | September | November |
| February | April | June | August | October | December |

Complete the sentences.

1. The second month is _____ .

2. My birthday is in _____ .

3. School starts in _____ .

The names of three holidays below do not begin correctly. Find the picture for each and write the name of the holiday correctly below it.

Memorial Day   thanksgiving   Columbus Day
flag day   Lincoln's Birthday   halloween

_____   _____   _____

_____   _____   _____

Write the name of a **special day** on the line.
Start with a **capital letter.**
Draw a picture of the special day on another paper.

mother's day   groundhog day   valentine's day
st. patrick's day   columbus day

1. Many people wear green.

_____

- -

_____

2. An animal sees its shadow.

_____

- -

_____

3. This day is named for a sailor.

_____

- -

_____

4. Candy hearts are given on this day.

_____

- -

_____

5. This is a special day for someone in the family.

_____

- -

_____

Circle the first letter of a name for a street, drive, avenue, or road.
Write each **street name** on a line. Start with a **capital letter.** Cut and paste the pictures by the right sentences.

1. The house is on dogwood drive.

   _____

   -

2. My school is on worker road.

   _____

   -

3. The store is at 13 ann avenue.

   _____

   -

4. Let's go to the park on tenth street.

   _____

   -

Circle the first letter in the names of **cities** and **states.**
Write the **capital letter** above it.
Draw a line on the map to show where the airplane went.

The plane took off from denver, colorado.

It went to lincoln, nebraska, and then to topeka, kansas.

After that it went to jefferson city, missouri.

The next stop was in oklahoma city, oklahoma.

The plane landed last in austin, texas.

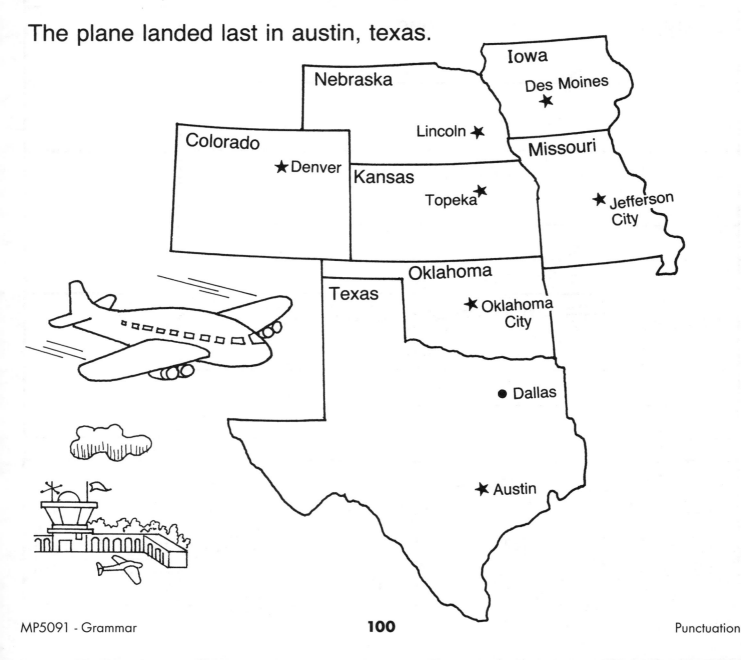

Name _____ Date _____

Circle the first letter in the names of **cities and states.**
Write the names on the lines.
Start each name with a **capital letter.**

1. Jojo lives in miami, florida.

_____

- -

_____

2. He will take a trip to portland, maine.

_____

- -

_____

3. Jojo will see his brother in madison, wisconsin.

_____

- -

_____

4. They will visit new york city, new york.

_____

- -

_____

Write the name of the city and state in which you live.
Find your hometown on a map.

Begin the names of **special places** with a **capital letter**.

Use the map to complete the sentences below.

| Tasty Bakery | Hill's Market | Pancake Place | | Oak Park |

Main Street

Union Bank

Odessa Library

Center School

_____

_ _ _ _ _ _ _ _ _ _ _ _ _ _ _ _ _ _ _ _

1. Mother buys cookies at _____ .

_____

_ _ _ _ _ _ _ _ _ _ _ _ _ _ _ _ _

2. Trees grow in _____ .

_____

_ _ _ _ _ _ _ _ _ _ _ _ _ _ _ _ _ _

3. Shana gets books from _____ .

_____

_ _ _ _ _ _ _ _ _ _ _ _ _ _ _ _ _ _

4. Sometimes we eat breakfast at _____ .

_____

_ _ _ _ _ _ _ _ _ _ _ _ _ _ _ _ _ _

5. We can buy apples at _____ .

_____

_ _ _ _ _ _ _ _ _ _ _ _ _ _ _ _ _ _

6. The name of the bank is _____ .

_____

_ _ _ _ _ _ _ _ _ _ _ _ _ _ _ _ _ _

7. The children ride a school bus to _____ .

EXTRA!

On another sheet of paper, draw a picture of your school. Be sure to write the name of your school somewhere in the picture.

The **first, last,** and **all important words** in a **book title** begin with **capital letters.**
Example: Stranger in the Storm

Read the book titles below. If a title is written correctly, color the book next to it red.

by C. Waters — Porpoises and Dolphins

by S. Care Stiff — mystery of the attic

by Mr. Rogers — new neighbors

by Hi Alps — Morning on the Mountain

by Stepen High — Step, Hop, Jump

by B. Quiet — state secrets

by Al Poe — bones the beagle

by I. M. Drowning — White Water and Yellow Rafts

Write the titles correctly.

1. leopard on the loose

_____

- -

_____

2. fire on bald ridge mountain

_____

- -

_____

3. the rainy day

_____

- -

_____

EXTRA!

Write the title of your favorite book.

The names of **special places** begin with capital letters.
The names of **days, months,** and **holidays** begin with **capitals letters.**
The **first, last,** and **all important words** of a **book title** begin with **capital letters.**

Find the words that need a capital letter. Color these spaces red. Find the words that do not need a capital letter. Color these spaces yellow.

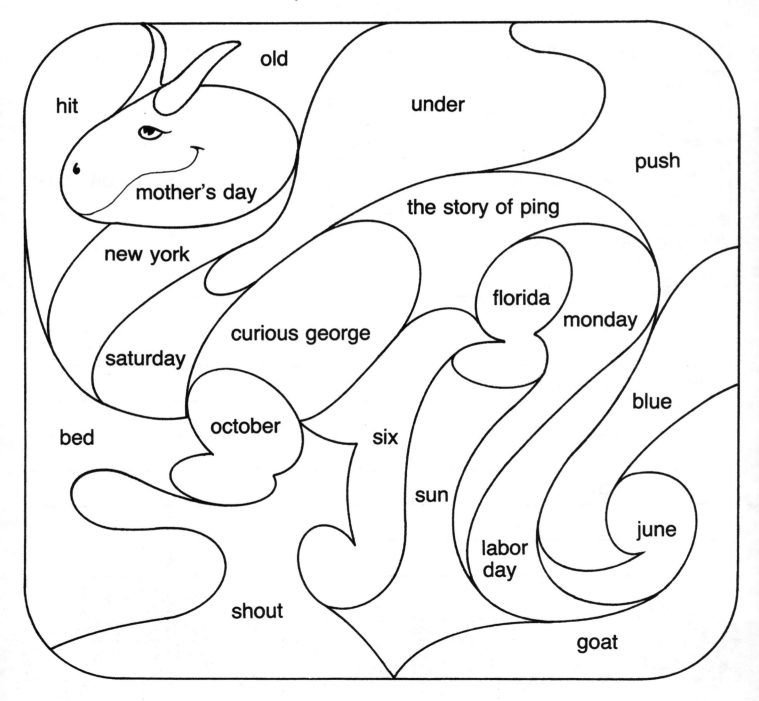

old

hit

under

push

mother's day

the story of ping

new york

florida

monday

curious george

saturday

blue

bed

october

six

sun

june

labor day

shout

goat

Circle each letter that should be a **capital letter**.
Write the **capital letter** above it.

dear michael,
    i am having a birthday party. it
is at 2:00 on saturday, may 5.
    it will be at my house at
6 dogwood drive.
    i hope you can come.
            your friend,
            josh

Write your answer to Josh.

_____

— — — — — — — — — — — —

_____

_____

— — — — — — — — — — — — — — — — —

_____

— — — — — — — — — — — — — — — — — —

_____

_____

— — — — — — — — — — — — — — —

_____

_____

— — — — — — — — — — — — — —

_____

EXTRA!
Draw a picture of the
gift you will bring to
Josh's birthday party.

Put a **comma** between the **day** and the **year**.
Put a **comma** or a **period** after the **year**.

1. Jane's birthday is on May 7 1980

2. I was born on October 22 1981

3. There will be a party on June 2 1988

4. May 10 1985 is when we got a dog.

5. August 1 1989 is when we will go.

Write a sentence to tell when something happened to you.
Draw a picture of it.

Use a **comma** between the **day** and the **year** in a date.
Use a **comma** between the name of a **city** and a **state.**

Omaha, Nebraska

Put a comma where it belongs in each date.

1. May 25 1961

2. February 1 1959

3. July 16 1984

4. March 26 1978

5. October 8 1985

6. June 12 1976

Write today's date. Remember the comma.

_____

- -

_____

Put a comma where it belongs in each address.

1. Hot Springs Arkansas

2. Akron Ohio

3. Danbury Connecticut

4. Boise Idaho

5. Fargo North Dakota

6. Portland Oregon

Write the name of your city and state. Remember the comma.

_____

- -

_____

Put a comma where it belongs in each sentence.

1. Abraham Lincoln was born February 12 1809.

2. He was born in a log cabin near Hodgenville Kentucky.

3. Lincoln later moved to New Salem Illinois.

4. He was elected President on November 6 1860.

Put a **comma** between the **day** and **month**.
Put a **comma** after the **greeting** and **closing**.
Write an answer to the note.

Thursday May 1

Dear Ken
　　Can you come to my house after school on Friday? We can play ball.
　　　　　Your friend
　　　　　James

Date: -

Greeting: _____

- - - - - - - - - - - - - - - - - -

_____

Body: -

_____

- -

_____

Closing: - - - - - - - - - - - - - - - - - -

_____

Name: -

_____

Write a note to thank someone for a gift.
Put a comma between the **day** and **month**.
Put a comma after the **greeting** and **closing**.

Date: _____

Greeting: _____

_____

Body: _____

_____

_____

_____

Closing: _____

Name: _____

Use a **comma** between **words in a series** to make the meaning clear.

Example: Ann Marie and Beth are friends.
(Without commas the sentence tells about two girls.)

Ann, Marie, and Beth are friends.
(With commas the sentence tells about three girls.)

Read each sentence. Put commas where they belong.

1. Kent has toast bacon and eggs for breakfast.

2. Teresa has cereal bananas and milk.

3. Kent Teresa and Don walk to school.

4. The day is cold cloudy and windy.

5. The children wear coats caps and mittens.

6. Don carries his paper pencils and pens in a bag.

EXTRA!

Think of three places you'd like to go on summer vacation. Write a sentence about these places, making sure to use commas.

Draw a line to match each day of the week with its **abbreviation.**
Write each abbreviation.
Start with a **capital letter.** End with a **period.**

Tuesday	Sun.	
Sunday	Mon.	
Wednesday	Tue.	
Monday	Wed.	
Saturday	Thu.	
Friday	Fri.	
Thursday	Sat.	

Write the names of the cities in ABC order.
Start each name of a **city** with a **capital letter.**
Put a **comma** between the names of the city
and the state.
Start the name of a **state** with a **capital letter.**

little rock arkansas   nashville tennessee

baltimore maryland   richmond virginia

dallas texas   atlanta georgia

1. _____

2. _____

3. _____

4. _____

5. _____

6. _____

Circle the **capital letter** and the **period** in each telling sentence.

1. A nest is in the tree.

2. Two little birds are in it.

3. Mother has food for them.

4. They can sing.

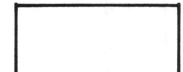

5. They will fly.

Cut and paste each picture by the correct sentence.

Write the **telling** sentences.
Start with a **capital letter**.
End with a **period**.

1. it will make a nest

_____

- -

_____

2. it will lay eggs

_____

- -

_____

3. it can fly

_____

- -

_____

4. it can get a bug

_____

- -

_____

EXTRA!

Draw a picture of the bird.

Write each sentence that **asks** something.
Begin with a **capital letter**.
End with a **?**.

the circus is here

may I go

will you go with me

may Tom go, too

can we get candy

the clown will be funny

A sentence that asks something is called a **question**. A question begins with a capital letter. It ends with a question mark.

The boys and girls ask questions.
Write each question correctly.

1.   what does he eat

_____

- -

2.   is he soft

_____

- -

3.   why do his ears droop

_____

- -

4.   what is his name

_____

- -

EXTRA! Color the picture of the dog at the top of the page. Answer each of the questions about the dog.

Circle the **capital letter** in the first word of each sentence.
Write a **.** or a **?** at the end of each sentence.

1. Is it big

2. It is big

3. You can see it

4. Can you see it

5. It can go fast

6. Can it go fast

7. Is it red

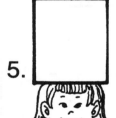

8. It is red

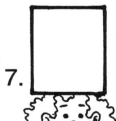

Cut and paste a to go on each who asks something.
Cut and paste a to go on each who tells something.

In a letter:
use a **comma** between the day and the year in a **date**.
use a **comma** after the **greeting** and after the **closing**.
begin each word of the **greeting** with a **capital letter**.
begin the first word of the **closing** with a **capital letter**.

Circle the correct letter part in each line.		
1. July 3, 1989	july 3, 1989	July 3 1989
2. Dear carlos,	Dear Carlos,	dear Carlos
3. your friend,	Your Friend,	Your friend,
4. Gary	gary	Gary,

Write the circled letter parts in the correct places.

_____

– – – – – – – – – – – – – – – – –

_____

_____

– – – – – – – – – – – – – –

_____

　　　　We visited the Science Museum today. We went
inside a real submarine. Julie and I got to look through
the periscope. I'm sending you a picture of the inside of
the submarine.

_____

– – – – – – – – – – – – – – – –

_____

_____

– – – – – – – – –

_____

A **command** is a sentence that gives an order.
It ends with a **period.**
An **exclamation** is a sentence that shows strong feeling.
It ends with an **exclamation mark.**

Read each sentence below. If the sentence is a command, write **C** in the box. If the sentence is an exclamation, write **E** in the box.

☐ It is windy!	☐ Here comes the wind!
☐ Button your jacket.	☐ It blew Laura's ball away!
☐ Put on a cap.	☐ Help her get it.

Write a command for picture A. Remember to end with a period.
Write an exclamation for picture B. Remember to end with an exclamation mark.

A.

B.

A. _____

B. _____

Name _____ Date _____

A good letter has correct capitalization and punctuation.

There are 11 mistakes in this letter. Put in three commas. Circle the eight words that need capital letters.

april 7 1989

dear ed
    thank you for visiting our class.
We liked the pets you showed us. i
liked the puppy best. he wagged his
tail.
       your friend
       alvin

Write the thank you note correctly on the lines below.

Answer Key

Page 3
People: boy, man, mother
Places: home, zoo, store

Page 4
School: (A) teacher
Firehouse: (C) firefighter
Airport: (B) traveler
Gas station: (E) driver
Park: (F) picnicker
Baseball diamond: (D) baseball player

Page 5:

Person:
1. baby
2. woman
3. girl
4. boy
5. man

Place:
1. school
2. store
3. library
4. park
5. zoo

Thing:
1. train
2. cow
3. window
4. car
5. book

Answers will vary.

Page 6
1. bird
2. feathers
3. tail
4. nest
5. fish

Page 7
1. present
2. presents
3. balloons
4. balloon
5. ribbon

Page 8:

Singular:
kite
teacher
table

Plural:
letters
monkeys
bats

Circle: book   cars   socks

Page 9

Singular:
doll   cow
bird   gym
fox   giant
book   coat

Plural:
babies   flags
eggs   girls
women   kites
pennies   sleds

Page 10
pueblos
houses, apartments, rooms
families, tribes, farmers
ceremonies, crops

Words made plural by adding es:
foxes, kisses, axes, punches, catches, wishes, lunches, buzzes

The plurals of the words that are not colored:
dogs, buttons, faces, pigs, nuts, houses, legs, farms, rabbits, hats

The hidden word is **CORN**, the Pueblo Indians' most important crop.

Page 11
1. seeds
2. fields
3. vines
4. birds
5. pumpkins

Page 12
horns
hats
cakes
games
toys

Page 13
1. house
2. Owls
3. sofa
4. brooms
5. stew
6. cape

Page 14
1. baby's
2. turtle's
3. sister's
4. beaver's
5. Eric's

Page 15:

Nouns: city, man, kite, glove, zoo, tree, book, banana, paintbrush

Verbs: see, make, sleep, eat, walk, draw, run, swim, go

Yellow: key, leg, pen, lip, cookie, truck, house, horn, bee, scarf, ax, tree

Black: doors, mice, boxes, bugs, apples, teeth, beds, zippers

Blue: all others

Page 16
Verbs:
play   throw   run   jump

Page 17
  A. **Run** fast.
  B. **Hit** the ball.
  C. **Throw** it to me.
  D. **Jump** rope.
  E. **Slide** down.
  F. **Sit** on it.

Page 18
  1. am
  2. are
  3. is
  4. are
  5. am
  6. is

Page 19
Across	*Down*
2. leaps	1. washes
5. climbs	3. swoops
7. jumps	4. dig
8. play	5. crawl
9. fly	6. swim

Page 20
sings, play	enjoy, cut	smiles
directs	paint, glue	says

Page 21
1. went	4. saw
2. were	5. were
3. was	6. see

Page 22
1. hear	4. liked
2. fly	5. followed
3. smelled	

Page 23
1. works	5. fly
2. worked	6. flew
3. buzzed	7. made
4. buzzes	8. make

Page 24
The **bold** sentence tells about the picture.
  1. The boy walks.
    The boys walk.
  2. **A rabbit hops.**
    Rabbits hop.
  3. A snake wiggles.
    Snakes wiggle.
  4. **A bird flies.**
    Birds fly.
  5. **A horse trots**.
    Horses trot.
  6. A dog barks.
    Dogs bark.

Page 25:
pulled	finish
cook	looked
laughed	listened
played	bark
open	painted
jump	walk
washed	fix
talked	fished

  1. walk   3. played
  2. listened

Page 26:
1. fell	5. ran
2. sat	6. grew
3. saw	7. got
4. ate	

Page 27:
1. does	2. do
3. do	4. does
5. do	

  1. You <u>did</u> not know her name.
  2. Michael <u>did</u> all of the painting.

Page 28:
1. have	4. has
2. have	5. have
3. has	6. have

  1. He <u>had</u> a broken arm.
  2. I <u>had</u> seven crayons.

Page 29:
1. were	4. was
2. was	5. was
3. were	6. were

were	was
were	were

Page 30:
1. is	4. is
2. are	5. are
3. am	6. is

He is; I am; Sue is
We are; She is; I am
I am; They are; You are

Page 31
1. an	**a** sole
2. an	**a** tuna
3. a	**a** pike
4. A	**a** catfish
5. An	**an** anchovy
6. a	**an** oyster
7. a	**an** angelfish

Page 32:

a	a	a
a	a	a
an	an	an
an	an	a

a	an	a
an	a	an

Page 33
1. Ben
2. bike
3. horn
4. Jan
5. Ben, Jan
6. circus

Page 34
1. Mary, Bob, I
2. slide
3. swings
4. Bob
5. Mary
6. park

Page 35
1. I   5. I
2. I   6. me
3. I   7. I
4. me

Page 36:
1. This   4. Those
2. these   5. that
3. That   6. those

this book, those books
that dress, these dresses

those bears, that bear
that table, those tables

this bird, these birds
these pens, this pen

Page 37
1. firewood
2. campfire
3. pancake
4. tablespoon
5. blueberries
6. outdoors

Page 38
1. I'll   4. we're
2. He's   5. don't
3. she'd   6. they'll

Page 39

is not–isn't	I will–I'll
does not–doesn't	he will–he'll
are not–aren't	they will–they'll
has not–hasn't	we will–we'll
will not–won't	she will–she'll

we are–we're
I am–I'm
she is–she's
they are–they're
he is–he's

1. (is not) isn't
2. (They are) They're
3. (They will) They'll
4. (does not) doesn't

Page 40:
Circle:
dark, cold,
red, good, soft, wet,
big, old, orange, hard

mouse: gray, soft, small
snow: wet, white, cold
sun: hot, yellow, big

Page 41:
1. yellow   5. purple
2. green   6. red
3. blue   7. orange
4. white   8. black

Page 42:
1. easy   7. tall
2. fat   8. huge
3. yellow   9. loud
4. fast   10. big
5. cold   11. fuzzy
6. flat   12. round

hard, soft
hot, sharp, round, cold

Page 43:
Color:
teddy bear, snowman
needle, mouse
cotton candy, sun

Page 44
1. slower   5. faster
2. shorter   6. fastest
3. tallest   7. smaller
4. longest

Page 45
1. jog
2. trail
3. forest
4. brook
5. cap
6. giggled

Page 46
1. thick
2. south
3. Winter
4. long
5. dark
6. stayed

hungry

Page 47
1. to
2. right
3. meet
4. red

to, two, too
there, their, they're
so, sew, sow

Page 48
frog	bad
log	glad
fly	fun
my	run
dog	sad

Page 49
train	skate
plane	state
car	go
far	slow

Page 50:
1. Birds fly.
2. Rabbits hop.
3. People talk.
4. Babies crawl.
5. Lions roar.

Page 51:
Dale	friend
Ted	bird
balloon	girls
Five cats	Babies
bike	father
Curtis	Belinda and Jan

Jimmy, my sister, Aunt Rita, the park, my pencil

Page 52
1. cup	4. ball
2. cups	5. kites
3. balls	6. kite

Page 53
1. A seal
2. An elephant
3. A tiger
4. Three horses
5. A man
6. Two clowns

Page 54:
The team won the game.
My bike rolled away.
A baby dropped its bottle.
The cook baked a cake.
The kite blew away from her.

By column:
writes a letter
sings very loudly

builds a table
ran away
jumped over it
ate a carrot

Page 55:
P	S	P
S	S	P
P	P	P
P	S	P
P	S	S

Answers will vary.

Page 56:
The boy hit the ball.	(left)
The ball hit the boy.	(right)
The mouse scared the cat.	(right)
The cat scared the mouse.	(left)
The hat was on the horse.	(left)
The horse was on the hat.	(right)
The seal ate a fish.	(left)
The fish ate a seal.	(right)

Page 57
I can make a house.
This truck is big.
The box is little.
I can eat here.

Page 58:
1. The girl had a red balloon.
2. Pelicans like to eat fish.
3. She read five books this month.
4. Eric has a black cat.
5. The ball went in the goal.

Page 59
Get a cake mix.
Mix it.
Bake the cake.
Eat the cake.

Page 60
1. We go to the library.
2. We read books.
3. We listen to records.
4. I have a library card.
5. May I borrow some books?

Page 61
The dog scared the cat.	(right)
The cat scared the dog.	(left)
The goat followed the boy.	(left)
The boy followed the goat.	(right)
A clown laughed at a girl.	(right)
A girl laughed at a clown.	(left)

1. Mark can fix it.
2. Rudy is here.

Page 62
We play soccer.
The field is long.
Heidi kicks the ball.
Our team scores.

Page 63:
Picture is an octopus.

Page 64
1. sentence
2. not a sentence
3. sentence
4. not a sentence
5. not a sentence
6. sentence
7. sentence
8. not a sentence

Page 65
1. We had a fire drill.
2. The bell rang.
3. Our class lined up.
4. We walked outside.
5. The school was empty.

Page 66
It is good.
I like it.
It is big.
I will get it.

Page 67
Here it is.
It is for you.
You can eat it.
This is for me.
I am full.

Page 68
1. I like dogs and cats.
2. We have candy and gum.
3. I will eat ham and eggs.

Page 69
1. My hands and feet are cold.
2. Anna and Michael can bake pies.
3. Cows and horses are in the barn.
4. The dog barked and growled.
5. Jenny can hop and skip.

Page 70
Statements: (red)
I went fishing.
The wagon is red.
She fed the kitten.
Hank paints a picture.

Exclamations: (orange)
Look out!
It's falling!
It burned my hand!
The lion is loose!

Questions: (blue)
Who is first?
Did he find it?
Is lunch ready?
Where is my shirt?

Commands: (green)
Put it here.
Close the door.
Open your book.
Wash your hands.

Page 71
1. **A** frog is smooth and shiny.
2. **It** has long legs.
3. **F**rogs lay eggs in clumps.
4. **T**he toad has rough skin.
5. **It** has short legs.

Page 72:
1. Can I ride on this? No
2. Is the monkey eating? Yes
3. Is this a bicycle? No
4. Is the boy running? Yes

Page 73:
Who is your teacher?
What is your name?
When is your birthday?
Where do you live?
Why are you sad?

what	who
where	what
where	when
who	when

Page 74
1. C   2. B   3. A   4. D

Page 75
1. We learn to read.
   We learn to sing.
   We learn to add numbers.

2. I can make a kite.
   I can make a picture.
   I can make cookies.

Page 76

Today we will go on a picnic.

Page 77

Sound travels in waves.
Our class made salt dough.
We had a Halloween party.

Page 78

The pelican has a special pouch in its bill.
The pouch can hold water. The pelican uses it as a scoop to catch fish.

Page 79

Stories will vary but should follow picture sequence.

Page 80

Felicia likes to bring her lunch to school. She can pack her favorite foods. She doesn't have to stand in line for a tray.

The line that does not belong in this paragraph is:
Whales are larger than elephants.

Page 81

Date: March 25, 1989
Greeting: Dear Kim,
Body: We moved into our new house on Friday.
I have my own bedroom. Mom says I have to keep it clean. Guess I'll have to learn to hang up my clothes and keep Scruffy off the bed.
Closing: Your friend,
Signature: Val

Page 82

Return address goes in upper left-hand corner of envelope.
Mailing address is written in the middle of the envelope.

Page 83

Information will vary.

Page 84

1. Althea	5. Kenny
2. Art	6. Kurt
3. Cora	7. Larry
4. Karen	8. Manuel

1. Say this tongue twister.
2. Sam sells skateboards.

Page 85

bark	jump
dog	pet
fun	wag
house	doghouse

Page 86

A bird flew in the window.
It landed on Pat's red table.

Page 87

1. Christmas
2. Easter
3. Fourth of July
4. Labor Day
5. Thanksgiving

Page 88

1. Ape Avenue	5. Happy Drive
2. Big Road	6. Lucky Street
3. Dandy Drive	7. Zoo Street
4. Funny Road	

Page 89

1 Mike (boy with cap)
2. Candy (girl with bow)
3. Ken (boy with basketball)
4. Pam (girl with long hair)
5. Beth (girl with doll)
6. Matt (boy with bell)

Page 90

Joe L. Brown
T.J. Jones
I.M. Good
Ann Crow
Champ
Puff

Page 91

Beth	Juan	Tony
Bandit	Boots	Polly
Harvey	Buster	Fluffy
Jared	Kim	Debbie
Ruby	Gretchen	Lois
Smoky	Denny	Duchess

Page 92

Mr. Wong	Mr. J.P. Ross
Miss Perez	Dr. C. Clark
Dr. Hollis	Miss R. Bell

Page 93

1. See what I am.
2. I can swim.
3. I can walk.
4. I can quack.
5. What am I?

Page 94
1. Sunday
2. Monday
3. Tuesday
4. Wednesday
5. Thursday
6. Friday
7. Saturday

Page 95
January	July
February	August
March	September
April	October
May	November
June	December

Page 96
1. It snows in January
2. We swim in July.
3. I can fly a kite in March.
4. We go to school in September.

Page 97
1. Sunday	1. February
2. Thursday	2. Answers will vary
3. Friday	3. Answers will vary

Flag Day, Halloween, Thanksgiving

Page 98
1. St. Patrick's Day
2. Groundhog Day
3. Columbus Day
4. Valentine's Day
5. Mother's Day

Page 99
1. Dogwood Drive
2. Worker Road
3. Ann Avenue
4. Tenth Street

Page 100
The plane took off from **D**enver, **C**olorado.
It went to **L**incoln, **N**ebraska, and then to **T**opeka, **K**ansas.
After that it went to **J**efferson **C**ity, **M**issouri.
The next stop was in **O**klahoma **C**ity, **O**klahoma.
The plane landed last in **A**ustin, **T**exas.

Page 101
1. Miami, Florida
2. Portland, Maine
3. Madison, Wisconsin
4. New York City, New York

Page 102
1. Tasty Bakery
2. Oak Park
3. Odessa Library
4. Pancake Place
5. Hill's Market
6. Union Bank
7. Center School

Page 103
Correctly capitalized book titles: Porpoises and Dolphins; Step, Hop, Jump; Morning on the Mountain; White Water and Yellow Rafts

Leopard on the Loose
Fire on Bald Ridge Mountain
The Rainy Day

Page 104
Words that need capital letters:
Mother's Day, New York, Saturday, October, Curious George, The Story of Ping, Florida, Monday, Labor Day, June

Page 105
Dear **M**ichael**,**
   I am having a birthday party. **I**t is at 2:00 on **S**aturday, **M**ay 5.
   It will be at my house at 6 **D**ogwood **D**rive. **I** hope you can come.

             Your friend,
             Josh

Page 106
1. Jane's birthday is on May 7, 1980.
2. I was born on October 22, 1981.
3. There will be a party on June 2, 1988.
4. May 10, 1985, is when we got a dog.
5. August 1, 1989, is when we will go.

Page 107
1. May 25, 1961	1. Hot Springs, Arkansas
2. February 1, 1959	2. Akron, Ohio
3. July 16, 1984	3. Danbury, Connecticut
4. March 26, 1978	4. Boise, Idaho
5. October 8, 1985	5. Fargo, North Dakota
6. June 12, 1976	6. Portland, Oregon

1. Abraham Lincoln was born February 12, 1809.
2. He was born in a log cabin near Hodgenville, Kentucky.
3. Lincoln later moved to New Salem, Illinois.
4. He was elected President on November 6, 1860.

Page 108

                                    Thursday, May 1

Dear Ken,
    Can you come to my house after school
on Friday? We can play ball.

                                    Your friend,
                                    James

Page 109

Thank-you notes will vary but must have capitals,
periods, and commas where necessary.

Page 110

1. Kent has toast, bacon, and eggs for breakfast.
2. Teresa has cereal, bananas, and milk.
3. Kent, Teresa, and Don walk to school.
4. The day is cold, cloudy, and windy.
5. The children wear coats, caps, and mittens.
6. Don carries his paper, pencils, and pens in a bag.

Page 111

Sun.–Sunday   Thu.–Thursday
Mon.–Monday   Fri.–Friday
Tue.–Tuesday   Sat.–Saturday
Wed.–Wednesday

Page 112

1. Atlanta, Georgia
2. Baltimore, Maryland
3. Dallas, Texas
4. Little Rock, Arkansas
5. Nashville, Tennessee
6. Richmond, Virginia

Page 113

1. **A** nest is in the tree.
2. **T**wo little birds are in it.
3. **M**other has food for them.
4. **T**hey can sing.
5. **T**hey will fly.

Page 114

1. It will make a nest.
2. It will lay eggs.
3. It can fly.
4. It can get a bug.

Page 115

May I go?
Will you go with me?
May Tom go, too?
Can we get candy?

Page 116

1. **W**hat does he eat**?**
2. **I**s he soft**?**
3. **W**hy do his ears droop**?**
4. **W**hat is his name**?**

Page 117

1. **I**s it big?
2. **I**t is big.
3. **Y**ou can see it.
4. **C**an you see it?
5. **I**t can go fast.
6. **C**an it go fast?
7. **I**s it red?
8. **I**t is red.

Page 118

1. July 3, 1989   3. Your friend,
2. Dear Carlos,   4. Gary

                                    July 3, 1989

Dear Carlos,
    We visited the Science Museum today. We went
inside a real submarine. Julie and I got to look through
the periscope. I'm sending you a picture of the inside
of the submarine.

                                    Your friend,
                                    Gary

Page 119

(E) It is windy!
(C) Button your jacket.
(C) Put on a cap.
(E) Here comes the wind!
(E) It blew Laura's ball away!
(C) Help her get it.

Sentences will vary slightly.

Page 120

Correct thank you note:

                                    April 7, 1989

Dear Ed,
    Thank you for visiting our class. We like the pets
you showed us. I liked the puppy best. He wagged his
tail.

                                    Your friend,
                                    Alvin